AF372985

The Dog on a Log

Story one in a series of bedtime stories told to my daughter...

by Phil Petranto

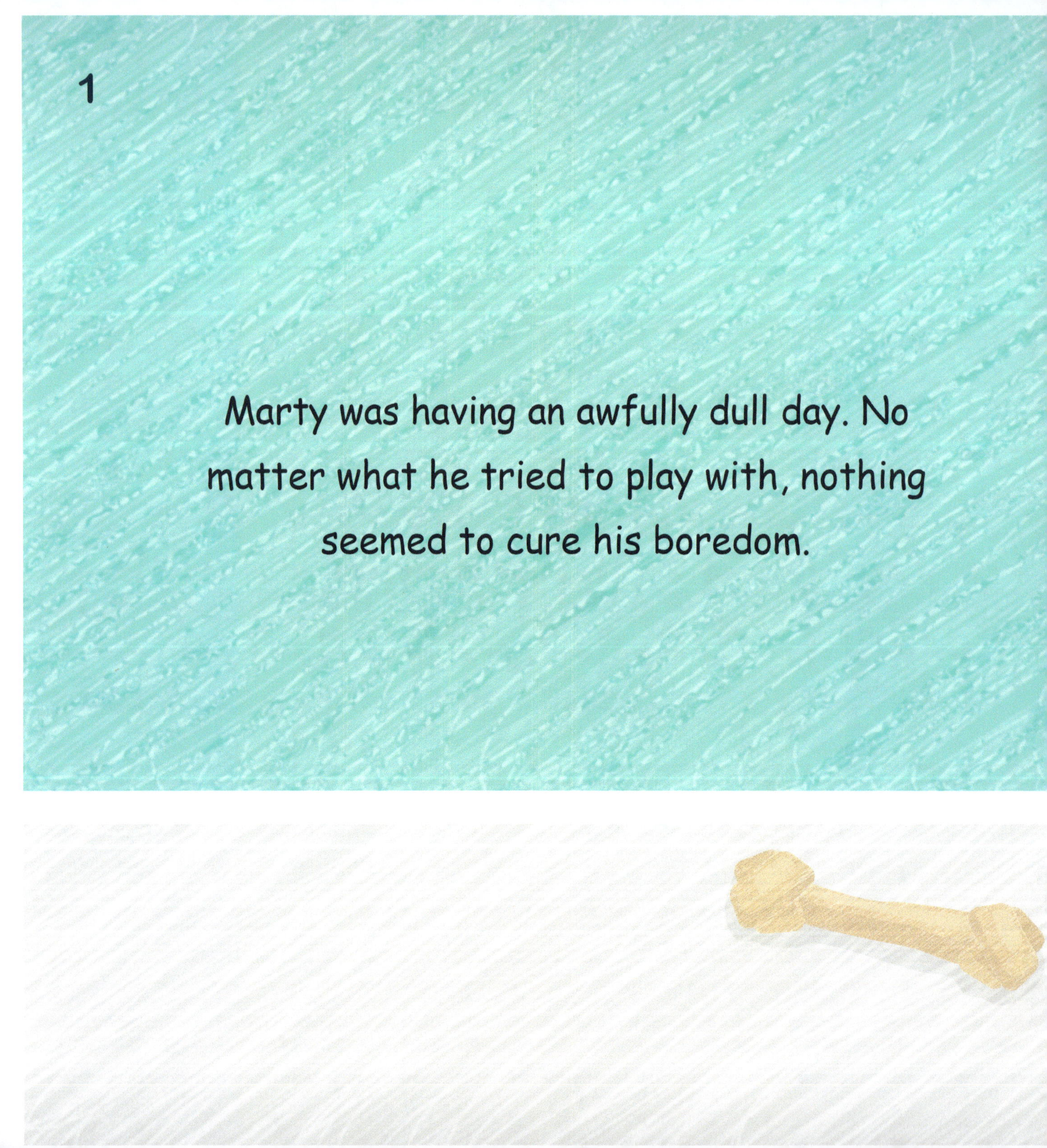

Marty was having an awfully dull day. No matter what he tried to play with, nothing seemed to cure his boredom.

He finally decided to go on an adventure!

Marty glanced back at the home where he and his loving family lived. He thought to himself, "I will be back later, but first, I'm off to explore!"

He couldn't resist the urge to wag his tail at least a few times.

Now, Marty was a curious fellow. His nose never missed any detail. He would always stop and smell the flowers. While passing through a local park, he sat and stared in awe at a mountain range in the distance.

It wasn't until he came across a river that he was halted in his tracks.

He thought to himself, "Hmm, if I'm to continue my adventure, I will have to get across this flowing water."

At first, he thought about swimming across, but the current was too strong. He looked around and came upon a log lying halfway on the land.

"Splendid!" he thought to himself. "Instead of trying to cross the river, I shall use this log to travel further on my adventure."

WHO

Marty took a few steps
back, then...

OSH!

He ran at full speed, jumping onto the log, setting it adrift. He howled with excitement as he quickly floated down the river.

He saw fish swimming, turtles sunbathing, and swans frolicking in the stiller parts of the water.

"This is great!" Marty thought to himself.

After some time, it occurred to Marty
that he was getting pretty far from home.

He wondered,
"How do I stop this log?"

"Hello there!" said a voice that seemed to
come from nowhere.

Marty looked around and said, "Hello?"

Emerging from the leaves of the tree, his friend Henry revealed himself. "Care if I join you?", the cat asked in an excited voice. Marty said, "Hey Henry! Sure, but I'm actually trying to figure out a way to stop this log ride." Henry then jumped from the tree branch onto the log.

Now, having a companion, Marty forgot about trying to stop the log ride. The two took in the scenery, paddling with their paws in the water.

"You two sure look like you're having a lot of fun. Do you have room for one more?" said a mysterious voice.

"Who and where are you?" said Marty.

There, on the shoreline, Marty noticed his good friend Felix, hopping up and down.

"Hi Felix!" said Marty.

"If you can get on here, you are most welcome, although I am trying to stop this log ride." With one great leap, Felix was aboard.

There they were, drifting down the river, telling jokes and splashing about.

Once again, Marty had forgotten about stopping the log ride.

The three were having a blast together, on what felt like a never-ending journey.

All of a sudden, Henry yelled out, "Look, the water disappeares up ahead!"

Marty looked, and saw what appeared to be mist. "This can't be good," said Marty. "We need to get off this river, and be quick about it!"

The three started splashing about frantically in different directions. This was getting them nowhere.

They had to think of something fast! Suddenly, Marty had an idea!

Marty thought to himself, "Instead of paddling with one or two paws, I shall use all four at once!"

Mimicking the doggy paddle, Marty laid flat on his stomach and told his friends to quickly get on his back. Then, with all his might, he started paddling toward the shore. It was working! Henry and Felix started yelling, "Faster Marty! We're almost at the end of the river!"

Then, at the very last minute, Marty's paws touched down on the river bed.

The log quickly slid out from beneath him and went over a high waterfall. With his friends still on his back, Marty waded back to shore.

After talking for a while, they all agreed that the day had been quite the adventure. Felix told Marty about a much easier place to cross the river to help him get back home. The sun was setting, so they decided to part ways and head to their homes before nightfall.

Marty was especially happy to be back on the ground.

Being a dog, he knew just how to find his way home, even though it was far away. He was just as excited to head home now, as he had been to explore earlier.

After getting settled in at home, he nestled down to sleep.

He dreamt about his exciting day, and
other possible future adventures.

THE END